INUYASHA

VOL. 33 VIZ Media Edition

STORY AND ART BY

RUMIKO TAKAHASHI

CONTENTS

THE STORY THUS FAR

Long ago, in the "Warring States" era of Japan's Muromachi period (*Sengoku-jidai*, approximately 1467-1568 CE), a legendary dog-like half-demon called "Inuyasha" attempted to steal the Shikon Jewel—or "Jewel of Four Souls"—from a village, but was stopped by the enchanted arrow of the village priestess, Kikyo. Inuyasha fell into a deep sleep, pinned to a tree by Kikyo's arrow, while the mortally wounded Kikyo took the Shikon Jewel with her into the fires of her funeral pyre. Years passed.

Fast-forward to the present day. Kagome, a Japanese high school girl, is pulled into a well one day by a mysterious centipede monster and finds herself transported into the past—only to come face to face with the trapped Inuyasha. She frees him, and Inuyasha easily defeats the centipede monster.

The residents of the village, now 50 years older, readily accept Kagome as the reincarnation of their deceased priestess Kikyo, a claim supported by the fact that the Shikon Jewel emerges from a cut on Kagome's body. Unfortunately, the jewel's rediscovery means that the village is soon under attack by a variety of demons in search of this treasure. Then, the jewel is accidentally shattered into many shards, each of which may have the fearsome power of the entire jewel.

Although Inuyasha says he hates Kagome because of her resemblance to Kikyo, the woman who "killed" him, he is forced to team up with her when Kaede, the village leader, binds him to Kagome with a powerful spell. Now the two grudging companions must fight to reclaim and reassemble the shattered shards of the Shikon Jewel before they fall into the wrong hands...

THIS VOLUME The fight for the last remaining Shikon Shard continues. Inuyasha is locked in mortal combat with the demon protecting the shard. Soon Naraku's presence will make things even more difficult. Will the arrow that Kagome received from Kikyo be enough to capture the shard?! Perhaps Inuyasha will have a new trick up his sleeve!

INUYASHA
Half-demon hybrid, son of a human mother and demon father. His necklace is enchanted, allowing Kagome to control him with a word.

KAGOME
Modern-day Japanese schoolgirl who can travel back and forth between the past and present through an enchanted well.

NARAKU
Enigmatic demon-mastermind behind the miseries of nearly everyone in the story.

MIROKU
Lecherous Buddhist priest cursed with a mystical "hell-hole" in his hand that's slowly killing him.

KOGA
Leader of the Wolf Clan, Koga is himself a Wolf Demon and, because of several Shikon shards in his legs, possesses super speed. Enamored of Kagome, he quarrels with Inuyasha frequently.

SANGO
"Demon Exterminator" or slayer from the village where the Shikon Jewel was first born.

SCROLL 1

THE WILL OF THE SHARD

DMMMM

WHO THE HELL ARE YOU...

...MAKING YOURSELF AT HOME ON MY FATHER'S BELLY?!

HSST...
KRIK KRIK KRIK

YOUR FATHER... YOU SAID...?

...KRAK
THEN YOU...ARE THE SON OF THE DOG GENERAL?

LORD INUYASHA. I WONDER IF THIS DEATH'S HEAD MAY BE...

IT IS I--
MYOGA!
YOU ARE
LORD
HOSENKI,
YES?!
...LORD
HOSENKI!

THE JEWEL-
SMITH WHO
CULTIVATED
THE BLACK
PEARL FOR
INUYASHA
...?
HO-
SENKI
...?

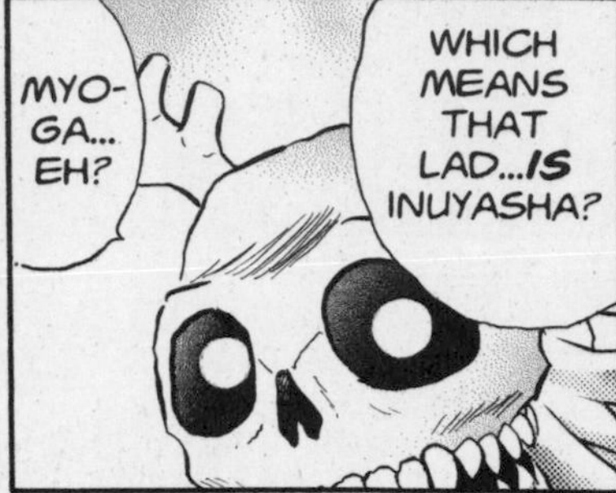
WHICH
MEANS
THAT
LAD...IS
INUYASHA?
MYO-
GA...
EH?

...
YES! YES!
HE IS NOT
YOUR ENEMY!

...BUT
INUYASHA...
TO COME TO
THIS REALM...
INDEED...I DID
CULTIVATE THE BLACK
PEARL FOR HIM...ON
HIS SIRE'S BEHEST...

WHY DID YOU BRING THE SHIKON SHARD HERE?!

!

THAT I CAN-NOT DO...

...FOR IT WAS THE WILL OF THE SHARD ITSELF...

...TO COME TO THIS PLACE OF DEATH.

!

THE SHIKON SHARD'S WILL...?!

I CAN HEAR THE VOICES OF MINERALS.
I AM A DEMON WHOSE SOUL IS LINKED WITH GEMS.

...A SHIKON SHARD CAME INTO MY POSSESSION.
WHILE I STILL LIVED BUT DREW CLOSER TO THE END...

THE CONCRETION OF SHARDS HAS BEEN IN THE HANDS OF EVILDOERS AND IS TAINTED.
IF THIS SHARD WERE TO COME IN CONTACT WITH THE OTHERS, IT TOO WOULD BE CONTAMINATED.
AND THE SHARD TOLD ME...
...THAT THE SHIKON JEWEL MUST NOT BE RESTORED!

IT CAME WITH ME...

...TO THIS GRAVEYARD OF DEMONS.

...

LORD INU-YASHA...

...IT WOULD BE WISE TO HEED HIM...

...AND LEAVE THE SHARD IN HOSEN-KI'S HANDS...

WHAT?! ARE YOU KIDDING?!

NARAKU GOT HERE A STEP AHEAD OF US!
HE'S HIDING SOME-WHERE-WAITING TO STEAL THAT SHARD!

I DON'T CARE WHO COMES...
KRIK...
...KRIKKL
I WILL NOT HAND IT OVER.

NOT EVEN TO YOU.
AND *YOU*... I WILL NOT PAR-DON.
KRIIIIK

WHOA!

KRAK

KAGOME, STAY RIGHT HERE!

INUYASHA!
WSH
HEY!
YOU OUGHT TO LEARN TO TELL FRIENDS FROM FOES!

RRRH!

IT'S USE-LESS, LORD INU-YASHA!
HOSENKI'S ARMS ARE AGGLOMER-ATIONS OF DIAMOND SHARDS!
MYOGA... WHEN DID YOU SWITCH OVER TO ME...?

CHINK

HO!
PHEW

VSSSH
FMP

IT SEEMS WE CAN'T REASON WITH HIM.

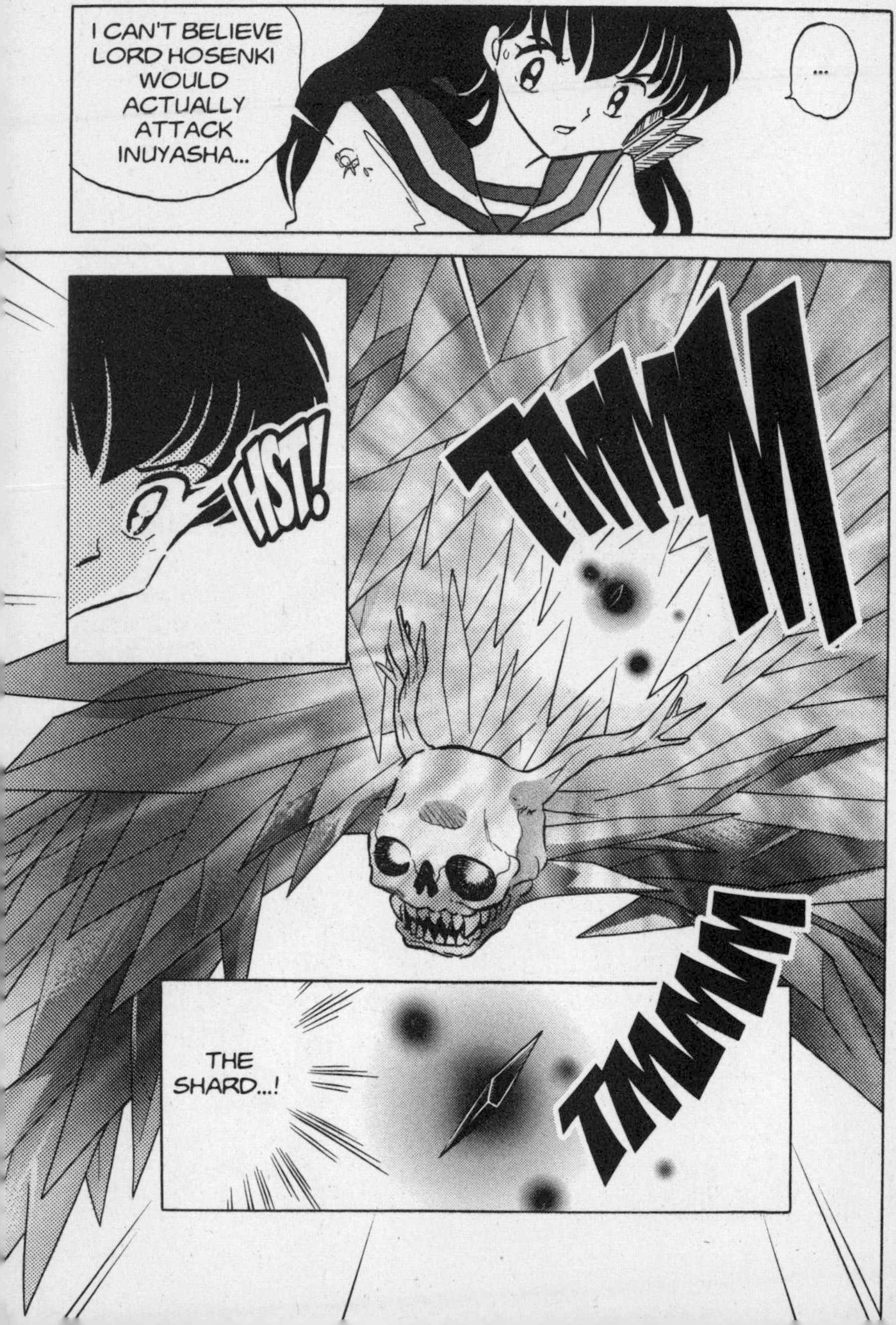

HST!

TMMMM

THE SHARD...!

TMMMM

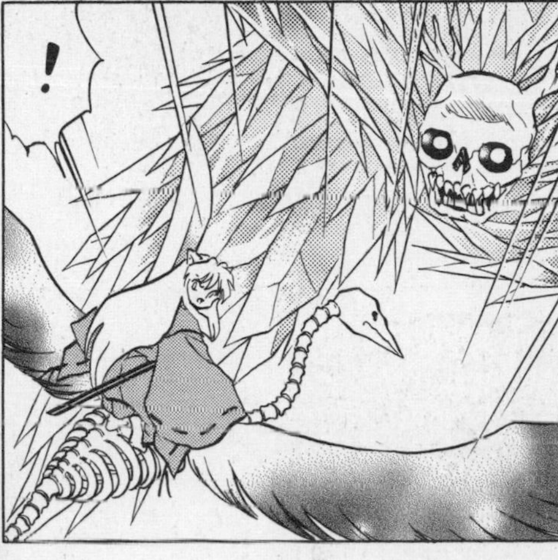
!

HOSENKI'S SHARD TURNED DARK!
BE CAREFUL, INU-YASHA!

A SHIKON SHARD CAN TURN GOOD OR EVIL, DEPENDING ON ITS OWNER'S SOUL.
WHAT'S GOING ON?!

!
...WO

...IT DOESN'T SOUND AS THOUGH HOSENKI BROUGHT THE SHARD HERE OUT OF ANY GREED OR SELFISH DESIRE.
BUT, FROM THE TALE HE TOLD...
WHICH MEANS ...

AND BY THE SIZE OF IT...
...IT'S NARAKU'S!
I SENSE ANOTHER SHARD...A TAINTED ONE...

...HOOO
...
LADY KAGOME...
...WHERE IS HE?!
SO NARAKU'S SHIKON SHARD IS CONTROLLING HOSENKI'S?

...I CAN'T ZERO IN ON HIS...!
THIS WHOLE AREA IS FILLED WITH EVIL AURAS...
I CAN'T TELL!

DID YOU HEAR THAT, HOSENKI ?!

IF YOU KEEP HOLDING ONTO THAT SHARD...

I WILL... NEVER... LET IT GO.

SCROLL 2

THE ARROW THAT FELL SHORT

COME ON, HOSENKI!
LET ME CUT THAT SHARD OUT OF YOU BEFORE IT EATS UP YOUR SOUL!
KRIIIIK KRIIIIK KRIIIIK

THE SHARD'S TAINT MUST BE SPREADING.
HIS WHOLE BODY'S TURNING DARK.
LORD HOSENKI WAS A GOOD FRIEND OF YOUR FATHER'S! HE IS *NOT* AN EVIL DEMON!
LORD INUYASHA, PLEASE GO EASY ON HIM!

YOU CAN TRY...

IF I CAN GO EASY AND STILL WIN...
...I WILL!

WIND SCAR!

WHOOOSHH
OH...!

SWOOSHHH

DID I
DO
IT...?

GLINT
!

WAH!

INU-YASHA!

KRAK
KRAK
!
TMP

NO MATTER WHAT ...
...I GOTTA GET TO THAT SHARD!

CHINK

HWRR
BOOMERANG BONE!

PYEW
YAH!
TAK TAK

TONG

I'VE GOT TO STOP HIS ATTACKS!

GLEEM...

THAT'S RIGHT...
...IF I CAN PURIFY THE SHARD...

KRIII
...I'M SURE MY ARROW COULD...

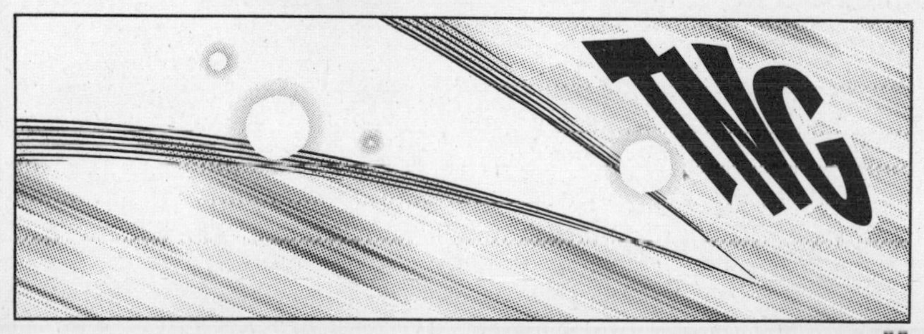
TING

IT HIT!
CHAK
HSSHHH
SSSSS
IT IS... USELESS...
TINK TINK

THE ARROW DIDN'T REACH THE SHARD!
THOSE SLIVERS ... THEY'RE LIKE ARMOR!
IT DIDN'T WORK...?!
HUH...?!

!

ZZAK
AHH!

LIKE KIKYO'S ARROW!
SHP

KIKYO'S ARROW... REJECTED HER?!

SSSS
WH... WHY...?

ALTHOUGH IT'S UP TO HER WHETHER SHE CAN MASTER IT OR NOT.
GIVE IT TO KAGOME.

CHNK
AUGH!
PHEW
IS IT THAT... KAGOME CAN'T HANDLE IT?!
WHAT DOES THIS MEAN?
!
KRIK KRIK
...KRIK
HE'S HIDING THE PLACE KAGOME'S ARROW HIT!

KAGOME ...
...SHOOT ANOTHER ARROW AT HIM!
HUH? BUT...
JUST DO IT!
O-OK.
KRIII...

CHOK

SO IF I
SLICE
THERE--

SSSS

WIND SCAR!
HSSSH
SHKKKKKK

HE BROKE THROUGH!

YES!
NOW I CAN GET THAT SHARD...

YOU... FOOLS...

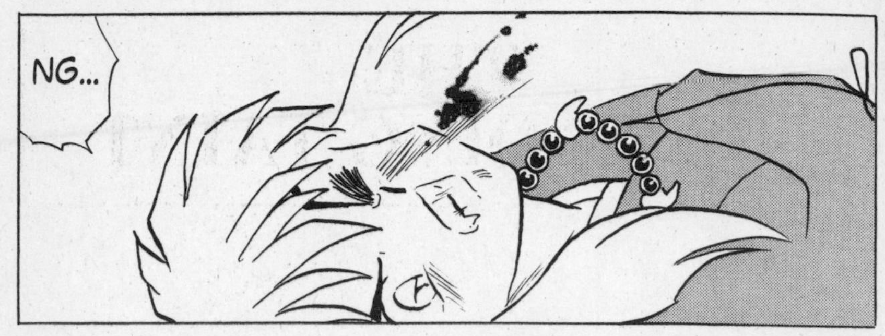
NG...

INU-
YASHA!

HWOOOO...

SSSS
FROM THE START, I...AND ALL OF YOU...

...HAVE BEEN MERELY PUPPETS...OF THE TAINTED JEWEL...

SCROLL 3
THE SPREADING TAINT

HERE IN THE LAND OF FIRE...
---HWOOO
...THERE IS A GATE TO THE *OTHER SIDE.*
SHUT UP.
YOU'RE THE ONES WHO ASKED ME TO GUIDE YOU HERE.
WH-WHAT DO YOU MEAN, KAGURA?
IS IT DAN-GER-OUS?
I'D RATHER NOT GET CAUGHT UP IN THE EXCITEMENT.
BUT I'M GOING TO EXCUSE MYSELF HERE.
I TOLD YOU I WOULDN'T GUARANTEE YOUR SAFETY.
WHAT?!

A GATE TO THE BORDERLAND BETWEEN THIS WORLD AND THE AFTERLIFE...

DO YOU WISH TO PASS?

DO YOU WISH TO PASS?

OR DO YOU NOT WISH TO PASS?

ULP?!

THE ONLY WAY TO PASS THROUGH THIS GATE...
...IS TO BE KILLED BY THE GATE-KEEPERS GOZU AND MEZU.

...

L-LORD SESSHŌ-MARU...!

WSH

HOOO...

WHOOSHHH
INU-
YASHA!

WRRR...

HEH HEH
HEH...SO
INUYASHA IS
DEAD...

I'VE BEEN WATCHING IT ALL...
WOOO

SO YOU... ARE THE POSSESSOR OF THE TAINTED JEWEL...?

KRIIIK

HISSSH

HE PIERCED NARAKU THROUGH HIS SHIELD!
!

WSS

KRIK KRIK

YES...I'VE HEARD YOU WERE A GREAT DEMON WHEN YOU WERE ALIVE...
...AND IT SEEMS YOU STILL HAVE SOME *BITE* LEFT.

KRAK KRAK
GLEEM

HE'S GOING TO TAKE THE SHIKON SHARD!

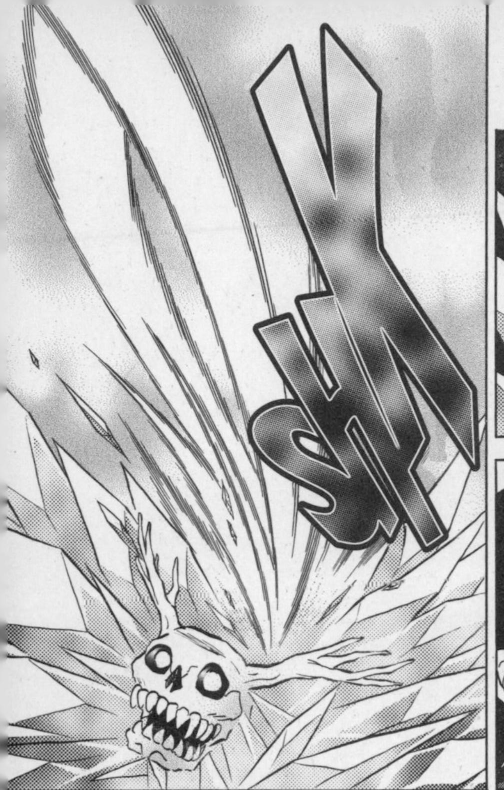

I'M NOT GOING TO LET YOU!
VSH

TNG

THE SHARD...
TURNED
PURE
BLACK?!
!

YEEEK!

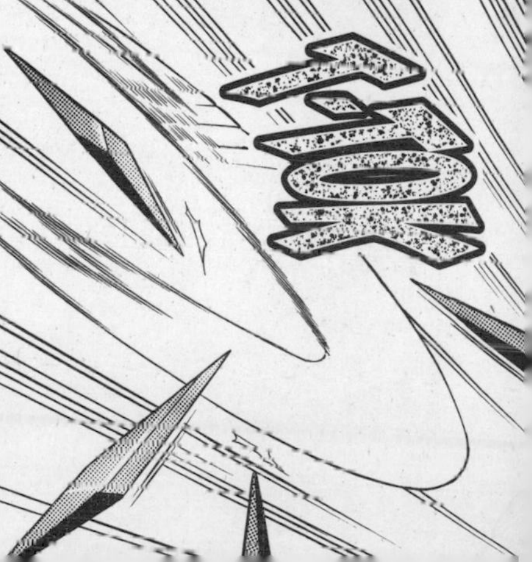

BOOM-
ERANG
BONE!
LADY
KAGO-
ME!

...IT'S SPREAD ALL THROUGH HOSENKI'S BODY!
THE SHARD'S TAINT...

HSSSH

T-TOK

AND IT'S ALL THANKS TO YOU.
SSSHH
HEH HEH HEH ...

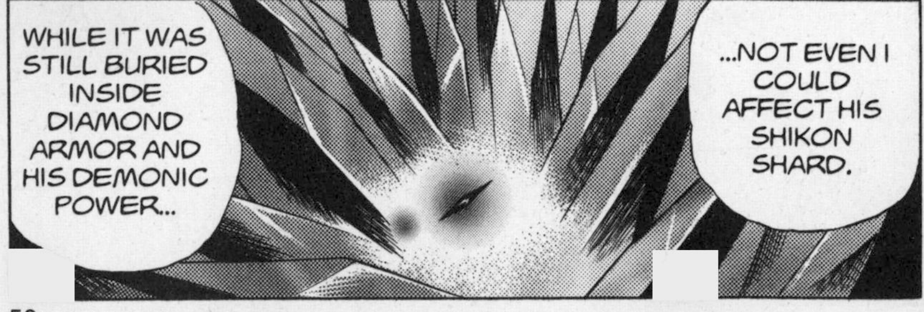
...NOT EVEN I COULD AFFECT HIS SHIKON SHARD.
WHILE IT WAS STILL BURIED INSIDE DIAMOND ARMOR AND HIS DEMONIC POWER...

ARE YOU SAYING OUR CRACKING HOSENKI'S BODY ALLOWED YOU IN?!

DAMN IT... PLAYED RIGHT INTO HIS HANDS...!
UGH ...

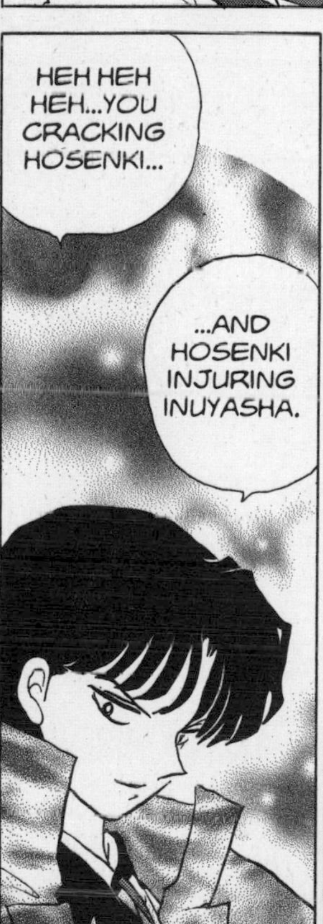
HEH HEH HEH...YOU CRACKING HOSENKI...
...AND HOSENKI INJURING INUYASHA.

THE SHIKON JEWEL SEEKS TO BE WHOLE...

KRAK KRAK
SHK...
I AM... ASHAMED ...

PF

FLAP

NARAKU!

FEH...

FWAP

PEH! YOU CELEBRATED PREMATURELY, NARAKU!
YOU GOT CARRIED AWAY AND SHOWED YOURSELF!

I'VE BEEN WAITING FOR YOU.
TMMMM

HE PLANS TO DRAG NARAKU OUT FROM BEHIND HIS SHIELD!
IT'S THE RED *TETSUSAIGA* ...!

PREPARE YOURSELF!

WHOOSH

SCROLL 4

THE UNBREAKABLE SHIELD

HYAH!

DOES INUYASHA... HAVE A FIGHTING CHANCE?!

THAT'S RIGHT. THE RED TETSUSAIGA ...

...WASN'T EVEN POWERFUL ENOUGH TO BREAK HAKUDOSHI'S SHIELD...

FSSH...

SHUT UP!
WIND SCAR!!

HOPE-
LESS.

KZT
BLOOB

HE'S PLANNING TO REFLECT BACK THE WIND SCAR!
AWP! EVERYONE-- RUN!!

IT WOULD BE SO FITTING FOR YOU TO BE CUT DOWN BY YOUR OWN BLOW...
FSH
HEH.

THERE'S... ONE LAST THING I HAVEN'T TRIED YET...

BLORP

BACK-LASH WAVE!

THE WIND SCAR...

...ENGULFED BY DEMONIC POWER... AND REFLECTED BACK?!

!

WOOOM

SHOOO
SSSSS
NO...
CHINK CHINK
NOT EVEN THE BACKLASH WAVE?!

HEH HEH HEH... POOR BOY...
...THAT'S ALL YOU HAVE, ISN'T IT?
SSSSS

B... BLAST IT...

ONLY THE DEAD MAY PASS THROUGH THIS GATE.

THOSE LIVING WHO WISH TO PASS...
...MUST DIE AT OUR HANDS FIRST.

HEH.
INTER-ESTING ...

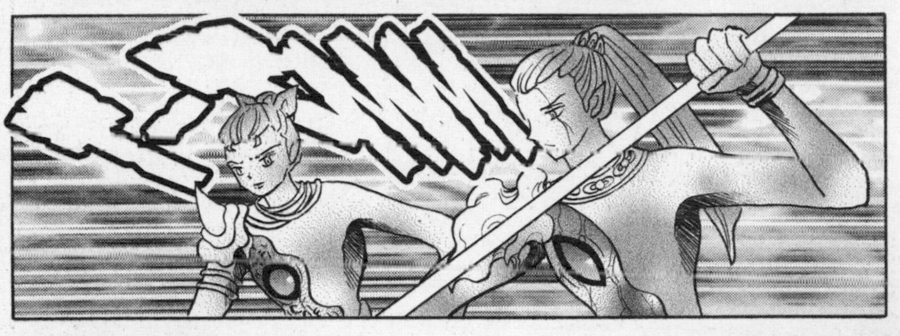

WSH

SCHAK

KRRP...
ULP!

LORD SESSHŌ-MARU, I KNEW YOU COULD ...
Y-YES!

THERE IS NO HOPE...
KRIIII...

SO... NOT EVEN SESSHŌ-MARU, HUH?

IT C-CAN'T BE...

TMMM

TENSEI-
GA...
TMMM

TMM
WE CANNOT BE SUNDERED BY ANY BLADE OF THIS WORLD.

SHIK

SO THAT'S WHAT IT IS...
HMPH.

TENSEIGA WAS TELLING ME TO USE IT...
FSSH

TMMM

KRIII...

!

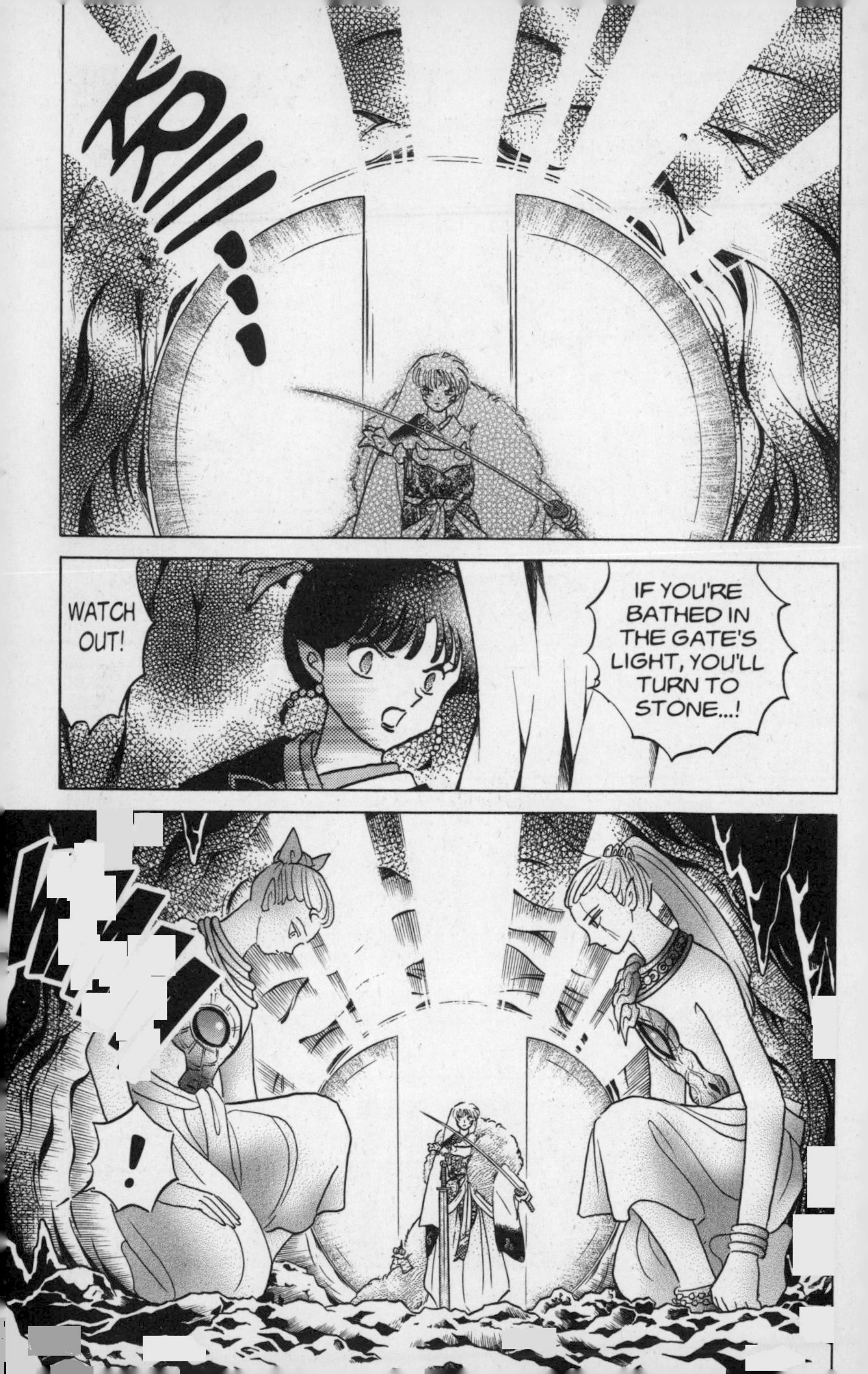

KRIII...!

IF YOU'RE BATHED IN THE GATE'S LIGHT, YOU'LL TURN TO STONE...!
WATCH OUT!

!

BEARER OF A BLADE OF THE AFTER-LIFE.
YOU MAY PASS.

EH?
TH-THEY'RE KNEELING?!

THUS, WE WOULD BE VULNERABLE AS WELL.
THAT BLADE CAN SUNDER THOSE NOT OF THIS WORLD.

ADMIR-ABLE.
CHK
"PICK YOUR BATTLES"... IS THAT IT?

TP

SESSHŌ-MARU **IS** THE ONLY ONE WHO CAN KILL NARAKU!
I WAS RIGHT ...!

SCROLL 5

THE FINAL SHARD

HOOOO
YOU'VE GOT NOTHING LEFT.
POOR LITTLE INU-YASHA...
NNGH...

YOUR TETSU-SAIGA...
...CANNOT CUT ME.

TO... HELL WITH YOU!

GRR...

THIS BATTLE'S... NOT OVER... YET!

SSSS

KRAK KRAK

SSSS

HE'S TRYING TO TAKE THE SHIKON SHARD!

!

BOOM-
ERANG
BONE!
WOOM

SHAK

WE CAN INJURE HIS BODY OUTSIDE HIS SHIELD!
YES!

BLOOP

WHA-?!
MIASMA!
SHHHH
BLPBLP
BLP

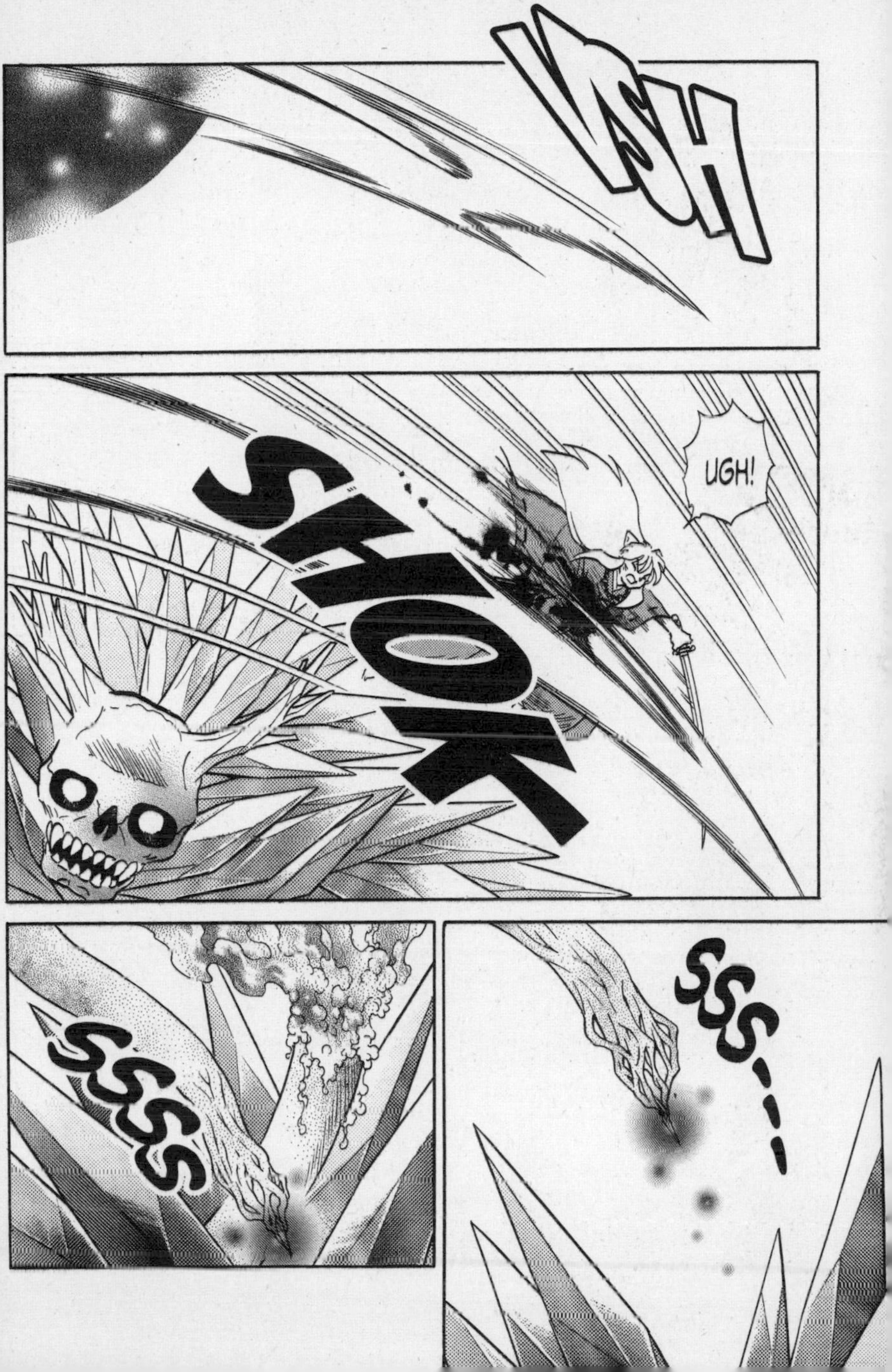

VSH

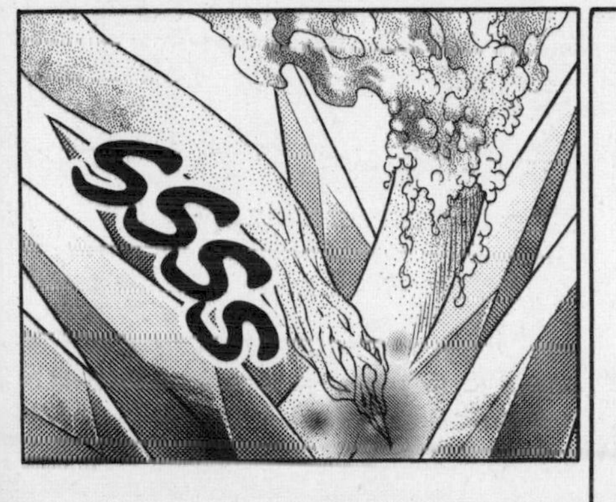

HEH HEH HEH...IT'S MINE AT LAST...
...THE FINAL SHARD OF THE SHIKON JEWEL!
THE... FINAL... SHARD?!
WRR
!

WAH!

MONK ...!
KLAK
WE WON'T LET YOU GET AWAY!

HEH...

I HAVE NO FURTHER NEED OF YOU ALL.
...SSSS

SAIMYO-SHO!
NO...! DON'T USE YOUR WIND TUNNEL!

HEH. YOU MAY CHOOSE.
WOULD YOU LIKE TO DIE RIGHT NOW FROM MY INSECTS' VENOM?

OR WOULD YOU RATHER LIVE...
...AND WANDER ABOUT THIS GRAVE-YARD FOR ALL ETERNITY?

WHAT DO YOU MEAN?!
?!

!

YOU HAVE NO WAY OF GETTING BACK TO THE WORLD OF THE LIVING.

THE ***RIVER OF BLOOD*** THAT BROUGHT US HERE...
...IS GONE. CLOSED OFF.

I SAID WE MIGHT NOT BE ABLE TO GET BACK!
I TOLD YOU SO!

...THEN ***YOU*** HAVE NO WAY BACK, EITHER!
IF THE PATH IS CLOSED, NARAKU...

...BUT I DO...FOR MYSELF ALONE...
HEH...

HE'S WAY TOO CARE-FREE...
TP...
I DON'T LIKE THIS...

IT'S ALL OVER.
DON'T YOU UNDER-STAND, INU-YASHA?
NARAKU...
DON'T THINK YOU CAN GET AWAY...
TM

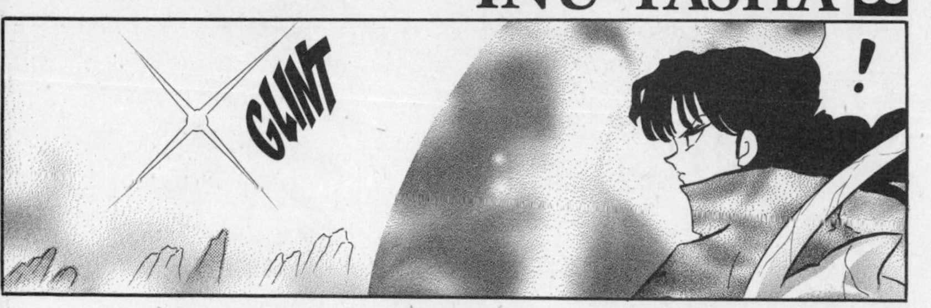
GLINT
!
VOOSH
DMMM
?!

HWOOO!!

SESSHŌ-
MARU!

...
...HOOO

EH...?!

WHAT A GENEROUS SIBLING.
DID YOU COME TO AID YOUR LITTLE BROTHER?

WELL. SESSHŌ-MARU.
HOW...HOW DID HE GET ***HERE***...?

HOOOOO

SHH...
!
SES-SHŌ-MARU...
...WHAT ARE *YOU* DOING HERE?

SHOOM

INU-
YASHA!
HUH...?!

UNGH...

WHAT ...
...THE HELL... WAS THAT...?
TM
INU-YASHA!

HOW DARE YOU-- A MERE HALF-DEMON-- VANDALIZE OUR SIRE'S GRAVE?!

SSS...

LORD SESSHŌMARU...!
DAMN... HIM...

HSSSH

!
L...LAD...

...STILL HAVE... STRENGTH TO FIGHT...?
DO YOU ...

?!

SCROLL 6
TESTED

HOOO...

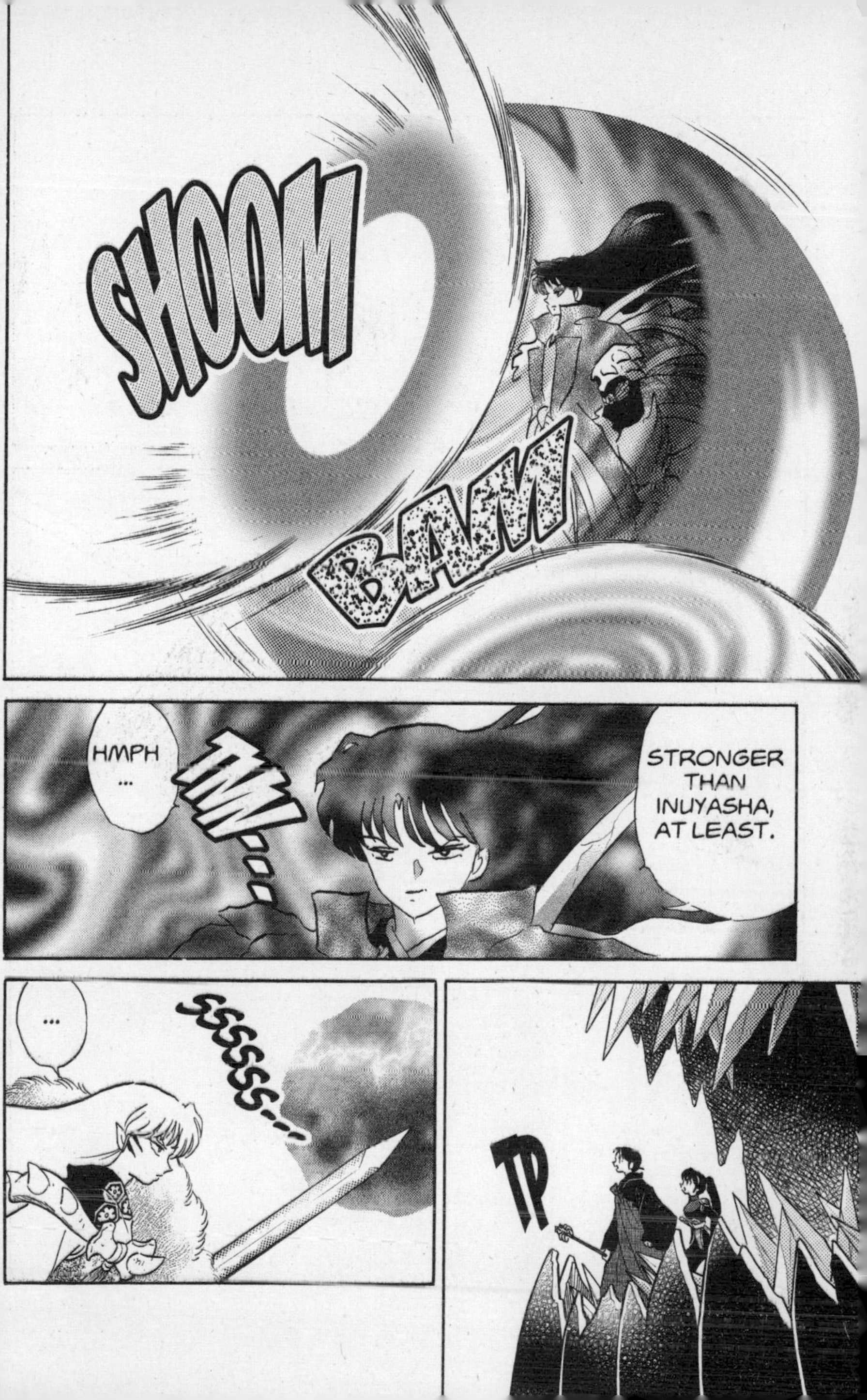

SHOOM
BAM

SO EVEN SESSHŌMARU'S POWER IS NOT ENOUGH TO DESTROY NARAKU'S SHIELD...

TOO SOON... THIS SHARD... WILL BE DRAWN...
...INTO THE TAINTED SHIKON... CONCRETION ...

?!

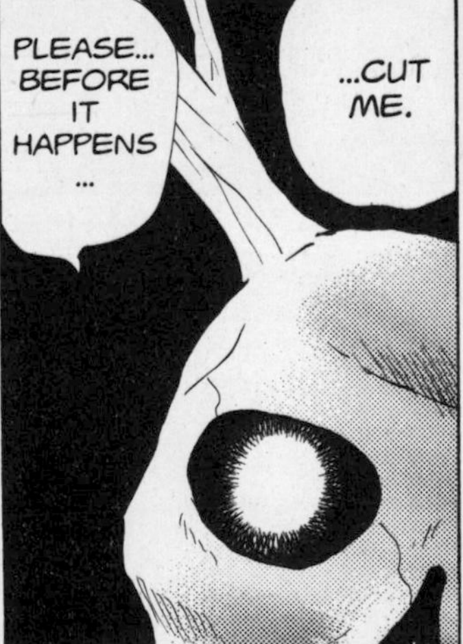
...CUT ME.
PLEASE... BEFORE IT HAPPENS ...

...YOU HAVE TO **TELL** ME THAT?!
DO YOU REALLY THINK...

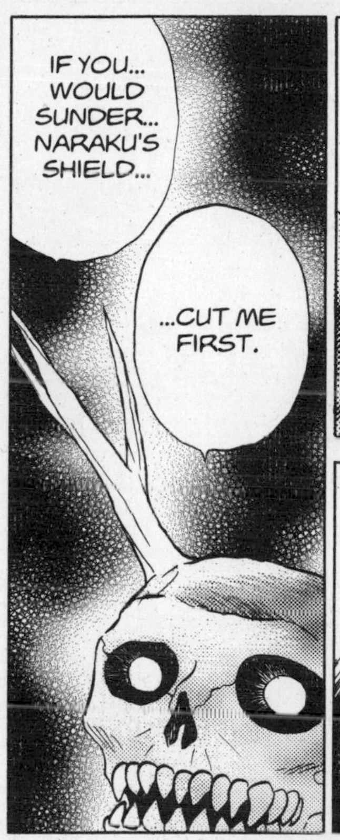
IF YOU... WOULD SUNDER... NARAKU'S SHIELD...
...CUT ME FIRST.

LORD HOSENKI ...!
YOU MEAN TO GIVE TETSUSAIGA DEMON POWER?!

THAT'S RIGHT! EVERY TIME THE BLADE DEFEATS A DEMON, IT GAINS NEW POWERS!
BUT ...

BUT THEN... WHAT'LL HAPPEN TO YOU?
BOY ...

YOU DON'T...HAVE THE LUXURY...OF WORRYING ABOUT OTHERS.
BE-SIDES ...

IF YOU ARE *NOT* WORTHY...OF POSSESSING THE SHARD...
...YOU WILL NOT BE ABLE TO CUT ME.
IN FACT...
KRIK KRIK
...YOU WILL LIKELY... LOSE YOUR LIFE.
SO BE PREPARED... TO DIE...
WELL... *THAT* MAKES ME FEEL BETTER.
LOSE HIS LIFE...?
STEP ASIDE, KAGO-ME.
INU-YASHA ...?

OKAY
...
SSS...
HYAH!!
SHAK

EH ...?!
FSH FSH

INU-YASHA!
TINY DIAMOND SLIVERS?!

PLUP
PLUP
GLINT
...
NOT EVEN A CRACK...?!
WHSH

OH, SESSHŌMARU. HEH.
YOU WANT TO DESTROY ME THAT BADLY?

THEN LET ME GRANT YOU YOUR WISH.
NARAKU...
...EXTENDING PART OF HIMSELF...?!

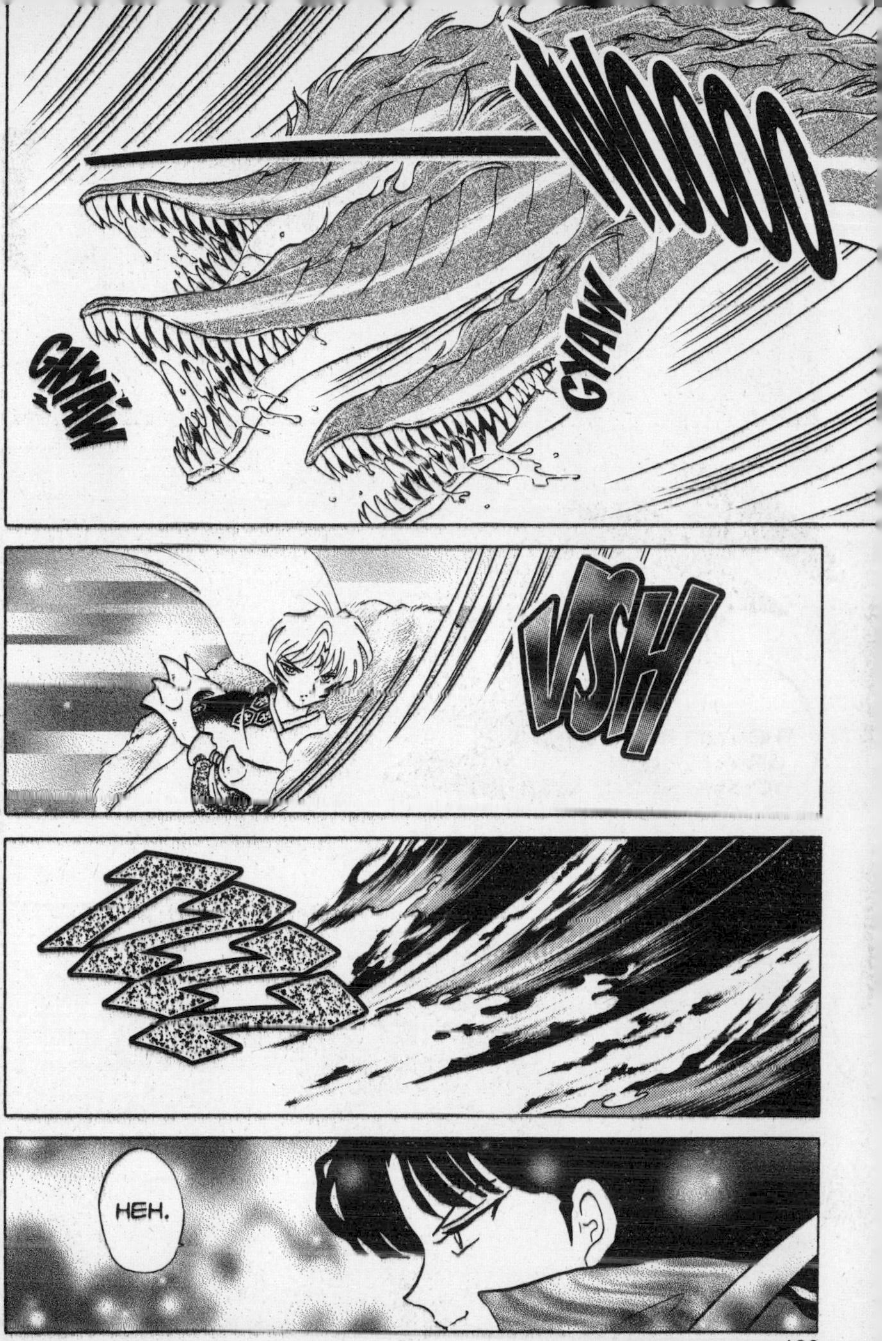

VWOOOO
GYAW
GYAAW

KAGOME!
GET BACK! IT'S A MIASMA!

YELP!
GLUB GLUB GLUB
SSSSS

SSSSS
!
L-LORD SESSHŌ-MARU!

!

SHHHHH

NGH!
AARGH!

EVEN IF YOU'RE NOT AF-FECTED ...
HEH.

...YOUR WATERY MIASMA CANNOT TOUCH ME.
HMPH ...

CHK
GET BACK!
I'LL PURIFY THE MIASMA!

VSSSH
TING

FEH.

I'M SAVED ...!
HEH HEH
I...I CAN BREATHE ...?

KRIK KRIK
KRIK KRIK

SO WHAT NOW, SESSHŌMARU?
EACH TIME YOU SLICE ME, MIASMA WILL BE RELEASED.

SOONER OR LATER...IT WILL KILL EVERYONE HERE.

L-LORD SESSHŌMARU...
DON'T WORRY! AS LONG AS WE HAVE KAGOME'S ARROWS--

BUT...WE DON'T.

THAT...
...WAS MY LAST ONE.

AND KIKYO'S ARROW... IS STILL REJECTING ME.

...THAT I WILL HOLD BACK MY BLADE FOR THE SAKE OF HUMANS!

VSSH

HERE COMES THE MIASMA!
ACK! JUST LIKE HE SAID...

FEH!

!

INU-YASHA!
I'LL BLOCK THE MIASMA!
HIDE AS FAR BACK AS YOU CAN!

SHUT UP!

THIS COMES FIRST!

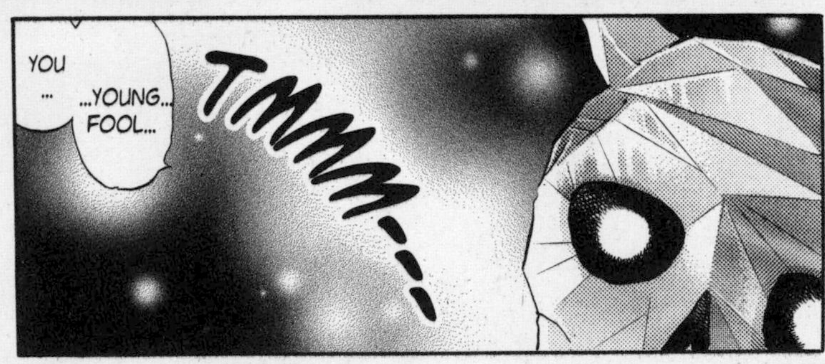

SCROLL 7

DIAMOND SPEARS

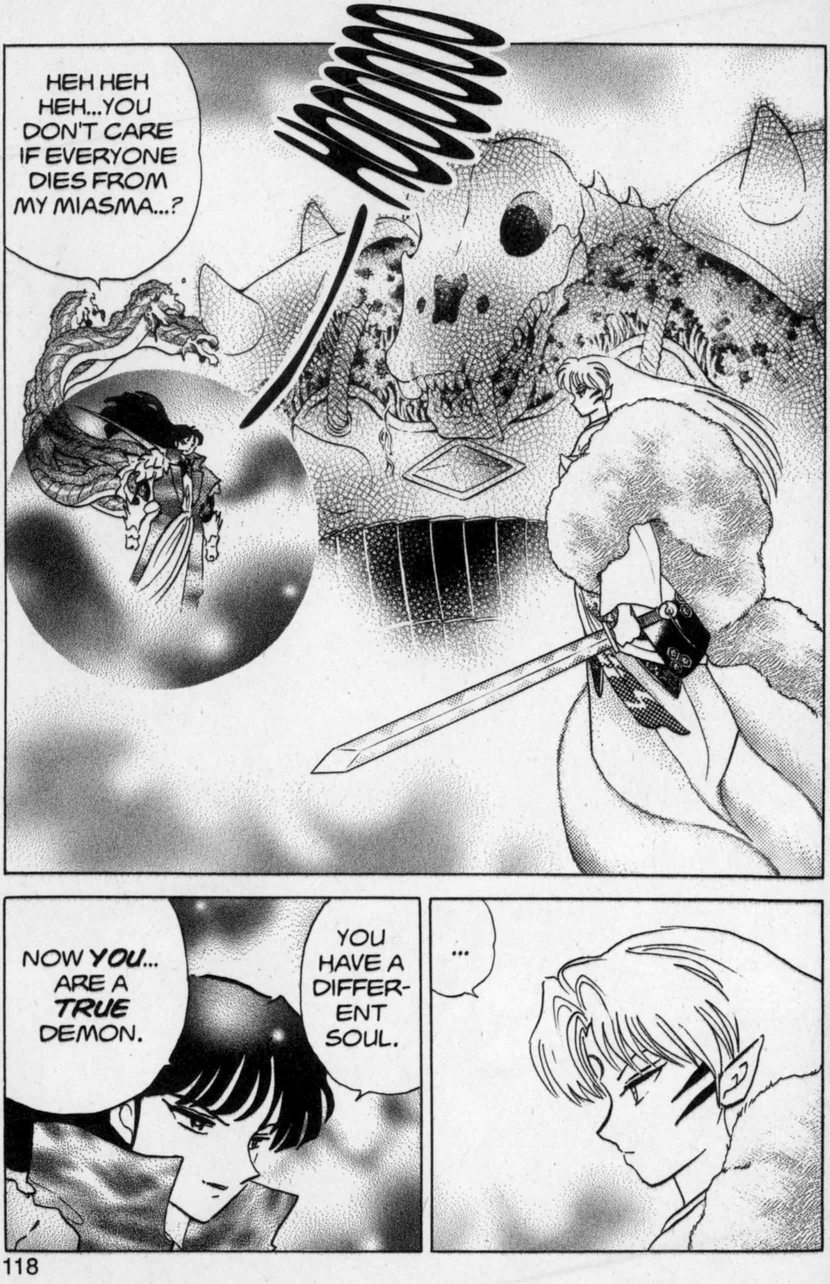

HEH HEH HEH...YOU DON'T CARE IF EVERYONE DIES FROM MY MIASMA...?

HWOOOOO
TM

SO...YOUR FRIENDS... ARE MORE IMPORT-ANT...
...THAN STRENGTH-ENING YOUR BLADE...?

...INDEED YOU ARE... ONLY HALF A DEMON...
I WONDER... IF A HALFLING...CAN EVEN MASTER...MY DEMONIC POWER...
HHHEE...

IF NOT-- THEN I DON'T NEED IT!
NO MATTER *HOW* GREAT YOUR POWER IS!

I JUST KNOW WHAT I HAVE TO DO-- RIGHT NOW!
WIND SCAR!!

SWEEPING THE MIASMA AWAY? HEH...
THAT WILL BUY YOU ONLY A FEW MINUTES OF...

!

EH...?! THESE ARE...
...HOSENKI'S DIAMOND SPEARS...?!

WHOOOOSH
FZZZ...

TETSU-SAIGA...!

IF YOU HAD BEEN GREEDY...
...AND CHOSEN TO STRENGTH-EN YOUR BLADE...

KRINK

TING
TING

...YOU'D HAVE BEEN KILLED...NOT JUST WOUNDED...BY THOSE SLIVERS...

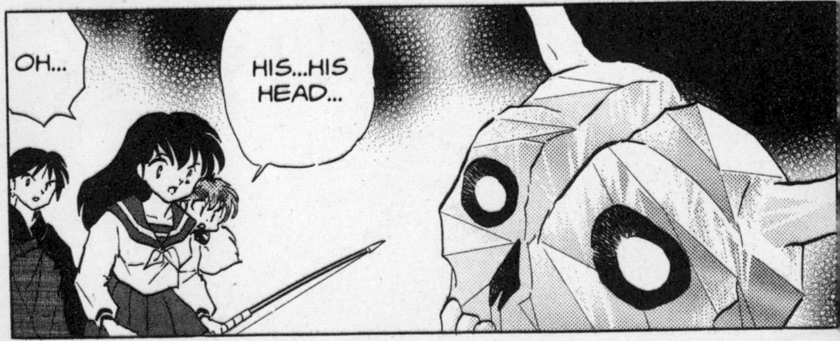
HIS...HIS HEAD...
OH...

INU-YASHA ...
...WITH YOUR HALF-DEMON SOUL...
...PLEASE ACCEPT MY DEMON POWER... KONGO-SOHA...

KONGOSOHA!

VSSH

NARAKU... YOU'RE DONE FOR!

TRY TO FEND THIS OFF!!

DID HE ACTU-ALLY...?!
YES! HE PIERCED NARAKU!

Y... YOU...
...SSSS

HSSSH

NO STRENGTH LEFT TO ERECT A SHIELD, MM...?

...FOR THE FINAL BLOW!

VSH

BOOM
FSSHHHH...
NNH ...

SHHH...
WAS IT ENOUGH ...?!

FZZ...

HE'S...FADING OUT?!

!
DMMM

SHH...

KIKYO'S ARROW...
DMM

THE SHARD STOLEN FROM HOSENKI!

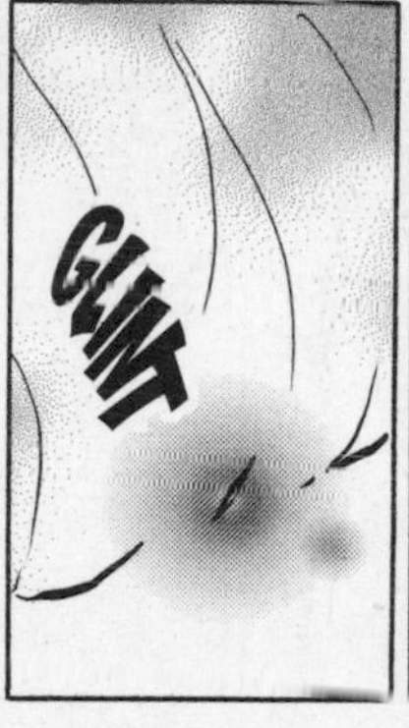
GLINT

I CAN DO IT!!
DMM

IT... WANTS ME TO USE IT NOW?
FP

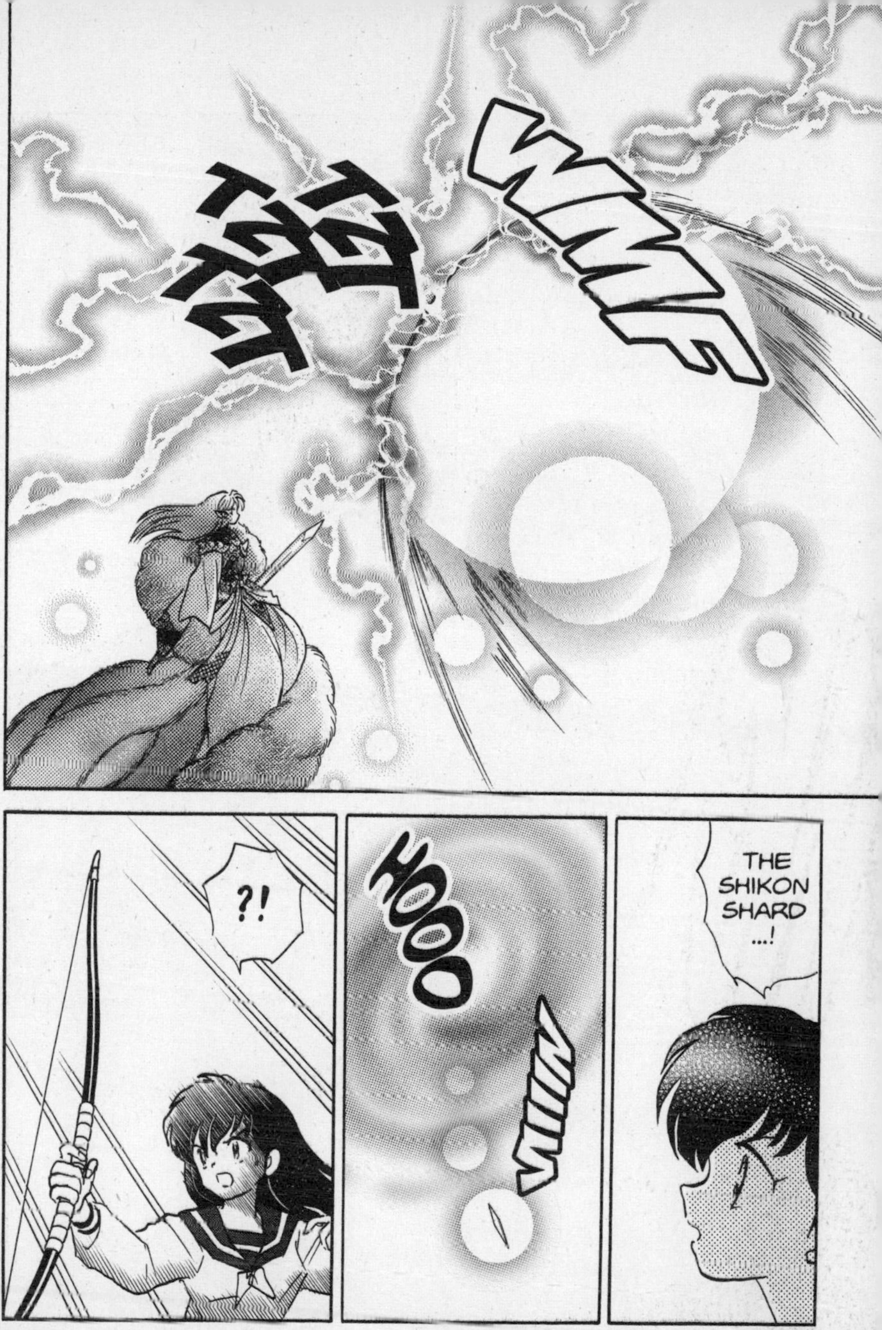

THE SHIKON SHARD ...!

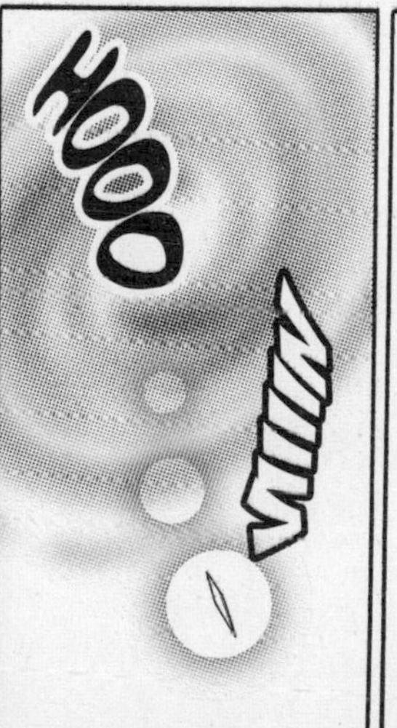
HOOO

?!

BUT NARA-KU...

PFFFF

...
...HE'S GONE ...!

IS IT CHASING AFTER NARAKU?!
KIKYO'S ARROW TOO!

SCROLL 8
THE WAY HOME

SSSH

HOW NICE IT WOULD BE...
...IF NARAKU DIES IN THE BORDERLAND.

GLEEEM
?!

BUT PROBABLY TOO MUCH TO HOPE FOR...
WOOSH

SSSS

KOHAKU!

A BARRIER ...?

WHAT'S HAKU-DOSHI UP TO?

KAGURA ...
...
NEVER MIND, YOU PROBABLY DON'T KNOW EITHER.

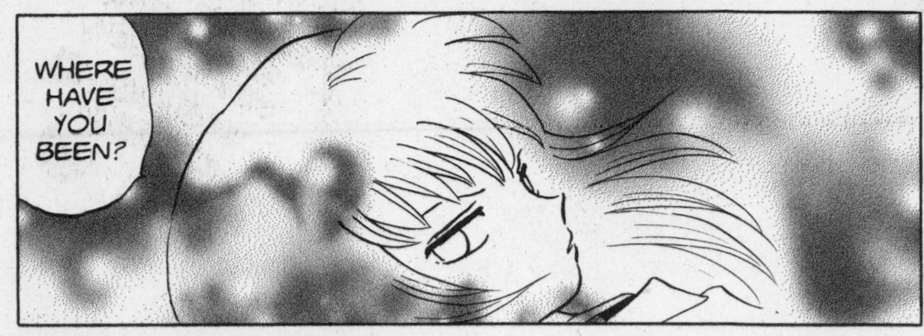
WHERE HAVE YOU BEEN?

TAKING A BREATHER.
I GET TIRED OF DRAGGING AFTER YOU ALL THE TIME.
...

ANSWER ME.
...YOU WERE AWAKE, HAKUDOSHI?

?!

WRRRR...
!

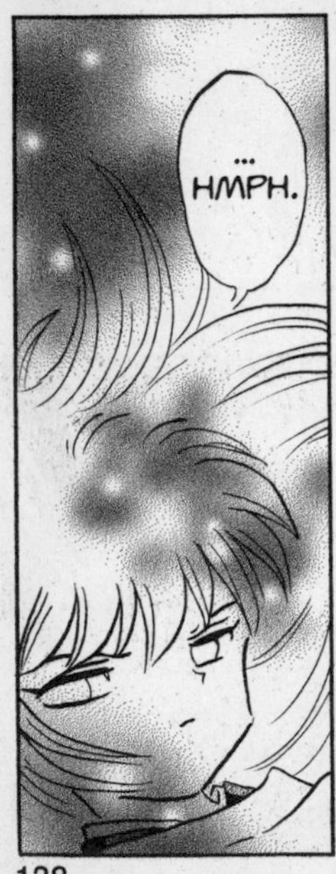
... HMPH.

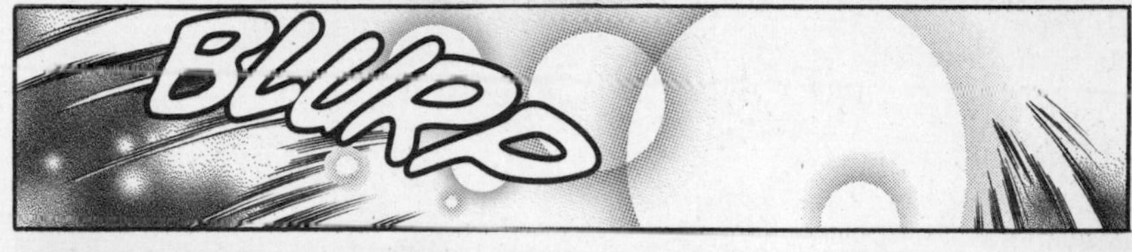
BLURP

VOOSH

...
N...
NARAKU ?!

SSS...
HOOOOO

THIS ARROW... KAGOME MAY HAVE SHOT IT...
...BUT ITS PRIESTESS POWER... IS KIKYO'S!

HOSEN-KI...

...WE'RE GOING TO TAKE THE SHIKON SHARD WITH US.

FINE... DO... AS YOU WILL...

I... WAS NOT ABLE TO PROTECT IT...
...I DID NOT THINK... SUCH EVIL WOULD COME...ALL THE WAY HERE FOR IT.

I COULD NOT END...
...THE BATTLE OVER THE SHIKON JEWEL.
NO ONE CAN END IT...
...AS LONG AS THE JEWEL EXISTS.

I DON'T KNOW HOW TO MAKE THE JEWEL DISAPPEAR...
...BUT...
...I CAN FIGHT BASTARDS LIKE NARAKU...WHO WANT TO TAKE IT.

THAT'S WHY, UNTIL NARAKU DIES...
...AND EVERYONE ELSE WHO WANTS THE JEWEL WITH HIM...
...I'LL CONTINUE TO FIGHT.
HEH... YOU CHOOSE... NOT TO HIDE THE SHARD...
...BUT TO STAND YOUR GROUND AND FIGHT... EH?
THEN GO. GO BACK...TO THE WORLD OF THE LIVING.
IF YOU DALLY... THE GATE SHALL CLOSE...

HSH---

SHUT UP! YOU'RE EMBARRASSING ME!
LORD SESSHŌMARU!!

LORD SESSHŌMARU! PLEASE WAIT!

...IT'S WHAT INU-YASHA SAID.
LORD MONK ...

WHY THE LONG FACE?
WHAT'S THE TROUBLE, SANGO?

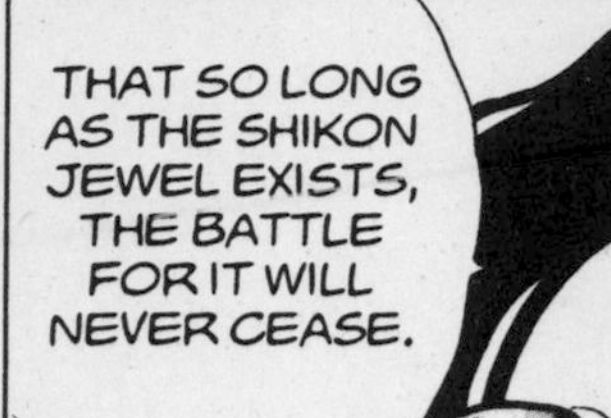
THAT SO LONG AS THE SHIKON JEWEL EXISTS, THE BATTLE FOR IT WILL NEVER CEASE.

BUT IF IT WERE TO DISAPPEAR...

YOU...ARE THINKING OF KOHAKU.

...

MY BROTHER IS STILL ALIVE BECAUSE OF THE SHIKON SHARD IMPLANTED IN HIS BODY.
IF THE JEWEL WERE TO DISAPPEAR... THEN KOHAKU...
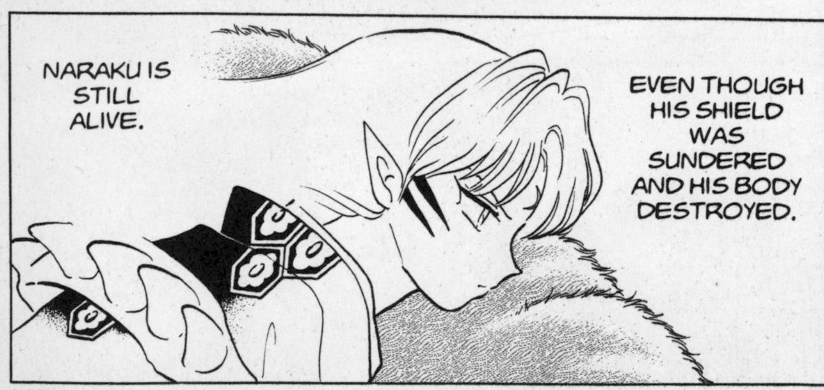
NARAKU IS STILL ALIVE.
EVEN THOUGH HIS SHIELD WAS SUNDERED AND HIS BODY DESTROYED.

WHERE IS HIS
HEART?!

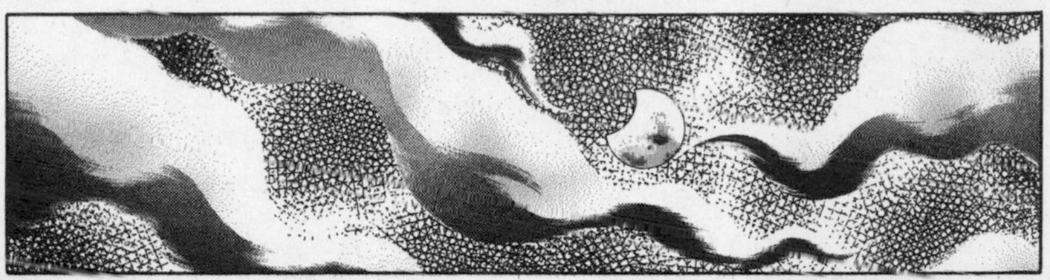

HOOO...
STILL NOT HEALED, HAKU-DOSHI?
SSSSS
IT'S THAT ARROW'S FAULT.

KIKYO IS ALIVE.

THAT WOMAN IS THE ONLY ONE WHO CAN IMBUE AN ARROW WITH SUCH POWER.

WHY HAVEN'T YOU KILLED HER?

I CAN'T SENSE HER AURA.

SHE'S DECIDED TO HIDE HERSELF COMPLETELY...

...WHICH MEANS... SHE IS NOT FULLY HEALED HERSELF.
SO NOW IS THE TIME TO DRAG HER OUT...AND FINISH HER.

THERE'S NO MORE DOUBT.
NARAKU'S- AND HAKUDO-SHI'S- HEART...

...IS INSIDE THAT CHILD...
...HAKUDOSHI'S TWIN.

NEITHER NARAKU NOR HAKUDOSHI EVER DIE...
...IS IT BECAUSE ... THEY ARE DEMONS?

HOW CAN I EVER DEFEAT THEM?!

HEY, KOHAKU.
YOU REALLY WEREN'T TOLD?

THAT BABY.
WHERE WERE YOU SUPPOSED TO TAKE IT AFTER THE CASTLE WENT DOWN?

THE BABY ...?
...I DON'T KNOW.

THAT'S RIGHT...HE HAD ME KILL EVERYONE IN THE CASTLE...
...IN ORDER TO GET THE BABY OUT.

WHAT WOULD YOU DO...
...IF YOU KNEW?

I KEEP TELLING YOU.
YOU'RE GOING TO DIE SOONER OR LATER, WHEN HE TAKES BACK THE SHARD INSIDE YOU.

UNLESS YOU KILL NARAKU YOU CAN'T SAVE YOURSELF!

AND I CAN KILL NARAKU...
...IF WE FIND THE BABY...?

KAGURA IS TRYING TO BETRAY NARAKU!

I DON'T...
...KNOW ANY-THING.
BUT...

...THAT *I'M* AFTER NARAKU, TOO.
THAT I'VE GOTTEN ALL MY MEMORIES BACK...

I CAN'T LET HER KNOW...

IF I GO ON PRETENDING TO SERVE HIM...

...ONE DAY, I KNOW... I'LL SEE THAT BABY AGAIN.

HAKU-DOSHI.

LURE KIKYO OUT INTO THE OPEN.

USE WHATEVER METHOD YOU WANT.

AND TAKE SOME-ONE WITH YOU.

HMMM...

SCROLL 9

THE SHRINE RAT

HAKUDOSHI...
KOHAKU...
...LURE KIKYO OUT INTO THE OPEN.

HSSH

CHK CHK CHK

CHK CHK

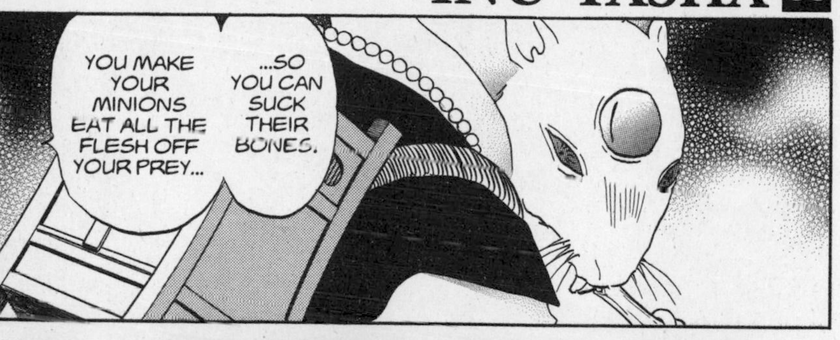

EH...?

SO YOU'RE THE ZUSHI-NEZUMI... THE "SHRINE RAT."

WHIR

EEP?!

HO.
NICE WORK, KOHAKU.
FSH
WUP

SURE.
HEFT THAT LITTLE ZUSHI ONTO HIS BACK AND COME ALONG.

YOU'LL DIE.
BE CAREFUL NOT TO OPEN IT, THOUGH.

TP

HSSH

INU-YASHA'S LATE.

KAGOME...MAYBE WE ***SHOULD*** HAVE GONE ALONG WITH HIM.

HE PROBABLY WANTS TO TALK TO KIKYO ALONE.

KAGOME, WHY ARE YOU ALWAYS SO GENEROUS?

INUYASHA'S SO MUCH TROUBLE...

ALWAYS SNIFFING AFTER HIS OLD MISTRESS, WAGGING HIS TAIL AT HER.

IT'S LIKE THE SAYING...FEED A DOG FOR DAYS AND IT'LL BE LOYAL FOR THREE YEARS!

I'M NOT A DOG.
BOOT

WHAT DID YOU TALK ABOUT?
... SO?

HUH?
...YOU DON'T HAVE TO LIE.

KIKYO... WASN'T THERE.

IDIOT.
WHY WOULD I LIE ABOUT THAT?

SIT.

I GUESS LADY KAGOME **WAS** HOLDING BACK.
STOP!
WOOOMP
YOU COULD AT LEAST TELL ME WHAT YOU TALKED ABOUT! SIT!
I WAS TRYING TO BE NICE, LETTING YOU GO ALONE.

HEY...!
THE NICE ONES ALWAYS SUFFER.
POOR KAGOME.

CHK CHK...

CHK
CHK
CHK

HUH?
SOME-THING'S COMING.

T-TM
T-TM
T-TM

H-HELP!
T-TMM T-TMM

CHK CHK CHK CHK

VSH
WHAT'S CHASING THEM?

WOOOOO
CHK CHK
CHK CHK

RAT DEMONS?!

INU-YASHA! DON'T!!
SANGO?!
!

SHUK

?!

THEY MULTI-PLIED?!

JUST AS I FEARED... SHRINE RATS!
CHOP ONE UP AND EACH CHUNK BECOMES A WHOLE NEW RAT!

SO HOW DO YOU GET RID OF THEM?!
WITH POISONOUS SMOKE!
...UNFORTU-NATELY, YOU NEED SPECIAL ***GRASSES*** FOR IT.

WOOOOO
THUP THUP THUP
THUP THUP THUP

YOUR VILLAGE WAS AT-TACKED?
Y-YEA...

LUCKY, THOUGH, ME AN' M'GRANDSON WERE UP IN TH' MOUNTAINS.
BUT EVERY-BODY ELSE...

SANGO ...
...YOU CALLED THEM... SHRINE RATS?

THERE SHOULD BE A BIG RAT SOME-WHERE... A MASTER.
HE KEEPS THE RATS INSIDE HIS PORTABLE SHRINE...
AND WHEN HE GETS HUNGRY, HE RELEASES THEM TO HUNT ANIMALS FOR HIM...AND PEOPLE.

BUT HE USUALLY NEVER HAS THEM HUNT MORE THAN HE CAN EAT.
I'VE NEVER HEARD OF SHRINE RATS SWARMING AN ENTIRE VILLAGE.

AND MORE ARE COMING.

I CAN SMELL THEM IN THE DISTANCE.
IT'S LIKE... THEY'RE GROWING IN NUMBERS, TOO.

CHK
CHK

CHKCHKCHK

THEY KEEP COMING, DON'T THEY?
HEH HEH HEH...

TMP...

CHK CHK CHK CHK
THEY'LL SPREAD IN ALL DIRECTIONS, POURING INTO THE HUMANS' VILLAGES...

R-RATS?!
CHK CHK

HOOOO

CHK CHK CHK CHK

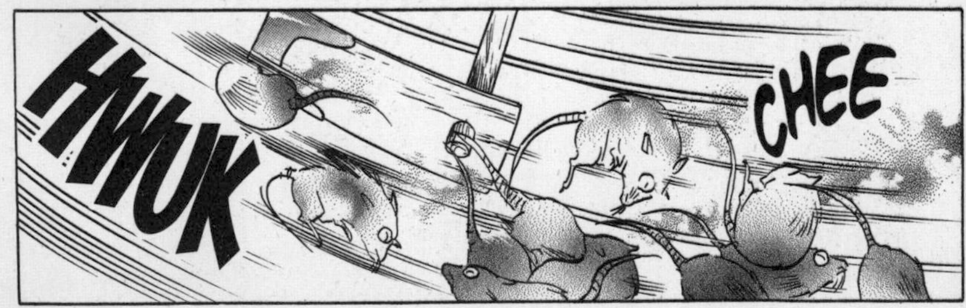
CHEE
HWUK

BLOOB
WHAT...?

AND WHEREVER THEY GO... THEY'LL KEEP MULTIPLYING.

CHK CHK CHK CHK CHK

... THAT'S RIGHT.
OH...

...DRAW KIKYO OUT?
AND THAT WILL ...

HEH HEH HEH... SOON, THIS ENTIRE LAND WILL BE OVERRUN BY RATS.

PRETTY SOON, NO ONE WILL BE ABLE TO IGNORE *THIS.*
IT WILL, DON'T YOU THINK?

ALL THIS... JUST TO CATCH KIKYO...

I SMELL 'EM!

WHAT THE HELL'S GOING ON?!
THIS RAT EXPLO-SION ISN'T NATURAL ...

SCROLL 10

THE DEMON LURE

THE SHRINE RATS ARE EVERY-WHERE!

SSHHHH

CHK CHK

SANGO, YOU SAY THE RATS MULTIPLY EACH TIME THEY'RE CUT?
YES.
NO VIOLENT ATTACK CAN HURT THEM... THEY ONLY REGEN-ERATE.

AND WITH THIS MANY OF THEM SCATTERED EVERY-WHERE...
...IT'S IMPOSSI-BLE TO TELL WHERE THEY CAME FROM.

BUT SOME-WHERE, THEY HAVE A HOME SHRINE?
MM-HM.
IT'S SAID THAT IF YOU DESTROY THEIR ORIGINAL ZUSHI, THE RATS WILL DISAPPEAR.

GLINT

MIROKU AND SANGO ARE LATE.

SHEESH ...
...WHY'D HE HAVE TO SEAL ME INSIDE THE SHIELD?

'CUZ WHEN YOU LOSE YOUR TEMPER, YOU START SWINGING TETSUSAIGA AROUND AND THAT'LL JUST MAKE MORE RATS!
DO YOU THINK I'M THAT STUPID?!

INU-YASHA, LOOK...!
HUH?

ZZZZ

THE WASPS!

WHICH MEANS THE RATS' RAMPAGE...IS NARAKU'S DOING!
FEH.
I FIGURED AS MUCH.

I NEVER DID BELIEVE HE DIED...

DID YOU THREE SEE THE WASPS TOO...?
YUP.

HEY! THEY'RE BACK!

WHAT DO YOU MEAN?

MORE THAT HE WANTS TO MAKE IT OBVIOUS THAT HE'S BEHIND THIS.

... NOT QUITE ...
DO YOU THINK NARAKU'S SENT THESE RATS AFTER US?

DOESN'T IT FEEL AS THOUGH HE'S TRYING TO LURE US OUT INTO THE OPEN?

OR PERHAPS...

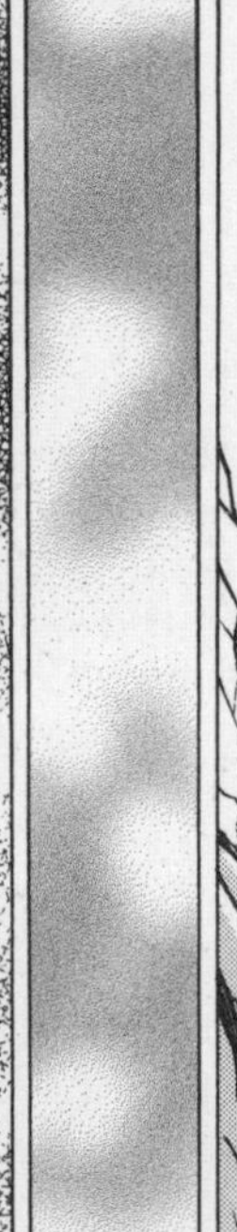

LADY KIKYO.
I HAVE BROUGHT YOU A BRANCH OF THE OGATAMA TREE, AS YOU ASKED.

HSH...

LADY KIKYO.
KOCHO HAS RETURNED.

...WE SHALL DESCEND THE MOUNTAIN.
THANK YOU. NOW, KOCHO, ASUKA...

TUP

SKTCH SKTCH

TK

SHOOOP
...
SHOOP
SHOOP SHOOP

THE RATS CHANGED DIRECTION...?!

COMING TOGETHER WITH THOSE OTHERS...

SSSHHHH

DEMON LURE?
I WONDER...HAS SOMEONE RAISED A DEMON LURE...?

YES... MERGING INTO ONE SWARM...
IT'S LIKE THEY'RE ALL HEADING TO THE SAME PLACE...

IT CAN ONLY BE DONE WITH SIGNIFICANT SPIRIT-POWERS.
A METHOD OF ATTRACTING ALL THE DEMONS IN ANY AREA SO THAT ONE MAY EXTERMINATE THEM ALL AT ONCE.

IS THAT WHERE YOU'RE GOING, RATS?!
POWERS... LIKE KIKYO'S...

LET'S GO, INU-YASHA.

KAGO-ME ...?

I'LL TRY TO LOCATE THE SHRINE.
SANGO ...

IT WORRIES ME...

...THAT THE FLOW OF RATS SEEMS UNENDING.

IT MAY MEAN THAT THE SHRINE IS CONTINUING TO RELEASE RATS.
SO UNLESS IT IS CLOSED... THEY'LL JUST KEEP COMING?

CHK CHK CHK

HEY, KAGO-ME!
IF WE'RE GOING TO SEE KIKYO...
...DOES THAT MEAN WE'RE GONNA SEE NARAKU TOO?
HUH...?

THAT'S... TRUE.
NARAKU WANTS KIKYO DEAD.

ARE YOU AFRAID OF NARAKU, SHIPPO?
YOU SHOULD HAVE STUCK WITH MIROKU AND SANGO.
NO WAY!
I'M MORE WORRIED ABOUT YOU AND KIKYO MEETING UP...
...AND POOR KAGOME'S HEART BEING BROKEN!

YOU'D BETTER TREAT HER BETTER THIS TIME!
YOU KEEP GOING AND I'LL THROW YOU OFF.

SHHH...
INUYASHA, OVER THERE...!
SHHH
THE RATS ARE... CLIMBING SOMETHING?!
CHK CHK CHK CHK

IT LOOKS LIKE SOME KIND OF TREE!
TREE ...?
WHAT TREE STRETCHES INTO THE CLOUDS ?!

HOOOOO
CHK CHK CHK CHK CHK
THE RATS ARE DISAP-PEARING UP IT...!
THIS MUST BE THE DEMON LURE!

SSHHHH

CHKCHKCHK

IT WAS.
BUT IT WAS IN THE RATS' PATH.
THIS... WAS A VILLAGE...

HURRY, KIRARA!
THMM
THIS IS SO BRUTAL ...

...IT SEEMS KIKYO'S MADE A MOVE...
KOHAKU, YOU STAY BEHIND HERE!

...
SHHH...

THEY LURED KIKYO OUT ALREADY ...
WHY ...?

AND DO **NOT** SHUT ITS DOORS!
GUARD THE SHRINE!
CHK CHK

HAKUDOSHI ACTS LIKE... THIS IS **FUN** TO HIM...

IF I SHUT ITS DOORS, THE RATS WILL STOP.

IT STILL MAY NOT BE TOO LATE TO SAVE A FEW PEOPLE, AT LEAST.

!

I'M BEING WATCHED...

IF I CLOSE IT...
...NARAKU WILL KNOW THAT I'VE GOTTEN MY MEMORIES BACK...

KOHAKU!

HSSST...

YOU...

...DID THIS...?

ZZZZ...

SISTER ...

TO BE CONTINUED...

TV SERIES & MOVIES ON DVD!

See more of the action in *Inuyasha* full-length movies